What's

?

*What is the insidious little object
that has infiltrated every household*

?

*What is adding to the anxiety
of an already frustrated world*

?

**IT'S RUBIK'S ROTATING NIGHTMARE
— THE CUBE!**

Now, it's time to fight back!

NOT
ANOTHER
CUBE
BOOK!

NOT ANOTHER CUBE BOOK

By W.C. Bindweed, David Godwin, and Mahood

BALLANTINE BOOKS · NEW YORK

ISBN: 0-345-30601-5
This edition published by arrangement with
Pan Books Limited, London

Manufactured in the United States of America
First edition: December 1981

Lyrics from the song "Mr. Rubik" by Robin S. Smith and Peter
Langford copyright © Warner Brothers Music/Autumn Music.
Printed by permission.

Designed by Gene Siegel

CONTENTS

1

THE CUBE:
A NEW THREAT
TO WORLD PEACE

The world is under threat from a new invader. It is only a few inches square, and can be twiddled round your little finger. It is the CUBE. Only a few years ago nobody had heard of the cube — it had yet to be invented. Then, from nowhere, Cubes started appearing in even quite normal households that had previously included nothing more dangerous than a bottle of aspirin and a copy of *The Joy of Sex*.

Do YOU recognize this object?

If so, you are under threat, and this book is for you.

Napoleon's Cube

The cube was supposedly invented in 1974, by a Hungarian called Erno Rubik. Hungary has already tried to conquer the world, in the time of the Tartars; this time it looks as if world domination will be complete. In 1980 more than five million cubes were produced, and soon the insidious object will have infiltrated its way into every house in the Western Hemisphere. It is probably no coincidence that the invasion of the Cube comes at a time of unprecedented economic recession: people are twiddling while industry grinds to a halt.

4

People buy the Cube thinking that it is going to be "fun." After three fruitless days of twiddling the thing they no longer care whether it is fun or not — they are hooked. Nobody seems to be immune from the attractions of Rubik's rotating nightmare: small children surrender to its charms with wanton abandon, oldsters fiddle with it in their wheelchairs. Books claiming to explain the secrets of its solution sell by the thousands. Yet nobody has realized that the Cube constitutes a threat to the very fabric of society as we know it! It is time to fight back against the Cube, to own up to the dangers it poses to our basic freedoms, like the right to do nothing on Sundays. Cube haters, unite!

It is rumored that Erno Rubik himself has made very little money from his invention (or so they tell us!). Do not be distracted by this. After all, nobody goes on about how much money Attila the Hun made from his attempt to conquer the world. The spread of the Cube is much like that of the Black Death, except that it does not require rats to carry it about from place to place. Like the flu, most of the Cubes come from Hong Kong. A few people seem to have natural immunity to the disease; Cubes just do not interest them. But most people are highly susceptible, especially those who first dismiss it as "a silly toy." When they get hooked they become really bad cases. The authors themselves were Cubaholics of this type.

Mathematicians tell us that there are 43,252,003,274,489,856,000 different color patterns you can get from the Cube, which is more than the population of China. Only one of these is the right answer. Small wonder that nobody can get the damn thing right.

Now there are a whole host of Cube gurus who go on about its mystical attractions and educational value. No doubt Sir Francis Drake said much the same about tobacco. People who have contributed to the literature on Cube solving are described as Cubemeisters. There are not many of these, and they have probably just found out a new method of cheating. In any case, the potential market for Cubes is 43,252,003,274,489,856,000. One of these is simply *bound* to come out right!

At a school near us there is a sign in the children's playground that says: "Only tennis balls and Rubik's Cubes allowed." This shows the extent to which even educators have been brainwashed

into regarding the Cube as an innocent, even beneficial, pastime. Have they failed to notice the bags under the eyes of those who were once their brightest pupils? We believe that the time has come to reveal the TRUTH about the Cube: it is DANGEROUS, ADDICTIVE, and nearly IMPOSSIBLE. Its use should be confined to consenting adults in private. We are not reactionaries. We realize that there are many already too deeply addicted to be suddenly taken off the "high" they have come to depend on. We have advice for them — and their families — later in this book. But the time has come to prevent the unrestricted advance of the Hungarian Horror, as *Time* magazine has termed it.

- The Cube at the moment carries NO HEALTH WARNING. Legislation should be introduced AT ONCE to make sure that every Cube carries the words: "Government Health Warning: This Cube will almost certainly destroy your brain."
- At the present time the Cube can be bought by any person of any age. There should be an immediate law passed to exclude its sale to all minors and dogs, and to anyone with naturally twitchy fingers.
- Cubes are often on blatant display where they are likely to cause offense to those with a sensitive disposition. Shops selling Cubes should have a warning sign clearly announcing the kind of wares they have available: "Anyone who is offended by explicit devices composed of twenty-six

Cubies, or by Actual Twiddling, should not enter these premises."

- Cube twiddling should be banned in public, where it might encourage others to take up the habit. Offenders should be put in good old-fashioned stocks — impossible to twiddle there!

These measures will be a start toward getting the epidemic under control. But things may have already gone too far for this to be enough. We are dedicated to the notion of a *Cube-free* world, where Man's fingers will be once more released to do those things they were designed for: operating machines, farming the earth, and doing intimate things with zippers.

WE HATE THE CUBE!

1. Nobody Can Do The Cube

People think that the reason they cannot do the Cube is that they are stupid. This is a myth circulated by nefarious manufacturers who want to sell yet more Cubes. People buy dozens of Cubes thinking that the next one will be easier to solve than the last one. Before we were cured, we used to have hundreds of Cubes around the house. Finally it was hardly possible to find a chair to sit on because they were covered in drifts of Cubes. And you know, NOT ONE of these hundreds of Cubes was solved!

The only people who can do the Cube are mathematical geniuses like Albert Einstein, and it is probably no coincidence that he is now deceased. Some of these mathematical geniuses are very young and get into the newspapers. People think: "If *he* can do it at thirteen, *I* can do it at thirty!"

This is a serious mistake. After all, Mozart could write symphonies when he was six, but how many symphonies have YOU written since last week? No, the plain fact is that the Cube is impossible for all those with an IQ of less than 349, which is 99.998 percent of the population.

2. The Cube Works Randomly

Every once in a while a Cube works out. This is because it operates on a principle of mathematics that states that once in a blue moon a coin will land heads up fifty times in a row. It is the same thing with monkeys at typewriters producing the works of Shakespeare: if you get enough monkeys sitting at enough typewriters sooner or later they will turn out a sonnet. This is just what the Cube is doing to the population as a whole: making monkeys out of us. People are so delighted to solve the Cube, they attribute it to their own intelligence. One man in Eugene, Oregon, was so exhilarated at getting it right (pure random chance again!) after two years of twiddling that he ran out into the street and was killed by a bus, which shows that success at this dangerous piece of apparatus is almost as risky as continuous frustration.

3. The Cube Is Addictive

It has been scientifically proved that addiction to the Cube can transform a balanced, no-nonsense individual into a drooling maniac. The final stages are pitiful to behold: shrunken wrecks of humanity lying motionless except for incessant twitching of the twiddling fingers. Yet Cubes are on sale everywhere to infants without any kind of health warning. We would not be surprised to find slot machines dispensing this mathematical time bomb in corner stores and youth clubs. More and more people are being recognized as Cubaholics — men and women whose lives are dominated by the Cube to the exclusion of all normal human emotions, like lust and the desire to make lots of money.

2

THE CUBE:
AN UNOFFICIAL
HISTORY

The Forbidden Cube

The Cube of Atlas

The Trojan Cube

The Stonehenge Cube

Nero and His Cube

Omar Khayyám

The Cube Excalibur

Sir Isaac Newton's Cube

3

CUBIC FACTS: THE HIDDEN HORROR

You may think we are overstating the dangers of Rubik's horrible little conundrum. But the FACTS are that the Cube has already caused a terrible toll of divorces, libel actions, piracy, distortion, extortion, contortion, and exhaustion. Here is just a sample of the many facts of the many-faceted monster that our investigations have brought to light. You may have heard of more. If so, please send the details to the headquarters of CHEAT (Cube Haters Extermination and Destruction) to add fuel to our campaign.

- It is a FACT that Cubes have enslaved some of the best brains in the world. The Massachusetts Institute of Technology now

has a whole battery of Cube-minded fanatics who even hold so-called Cube-Ins to try and capture the minds of others. Not content with the agonies of the standard "game," these Machiavellian mathematicians have invented new games that are EVEN MORE DIFFICULT!

- There are several books around that promise to tell you how to "solve" the Cube. One of these has been "pirated" — a totally illegal act — and there are court proceedings in progress about this. Surely no better demonstration is needed of the moral decay induced by proximity to the Cube.

- Fran Schmidt of Dusseldorf gave her husband Gundar a Rubik's Cube for Christmas. By February she was suing for divorce. "Gundar no longer speaks to me and when he comes to bed he is too exhausted from playing with his Cube to even give me a cuddle."

An Eyewitness Account of the Cube:

An old friend came to stay last week. He idly picked up my daughter's Rubik's Cube, which happened to be lying around. For the next two days, the Cube never left his hands except for meal breaks. I think he clutched it when asleep.

On the third day his wife hid the cube. But he was so upset and twitchy that she gave in, after first torturing him with a prolonged game of "getting warmer, . . . getting colder."

That night I came down late to find him filling a fat exercise book with pages of figures which, he explained, were in a notation he had invented for solving the cube. Unfortunately, we had not bought any of the little books on how to do it. And his notation turned out to be pitifully useless.

At the end of five days, the best he had achieved was one side out of the six. He could progress no further without jeopardizing this pitiful achievement.

I don't know where it will all end. I hate the horrible dull staring little object myself and have a near-superstitious dread of touching it. Even more, I hate the thought of that smug creep, Mr. Rubik, hanging out on his yacht in Budapest. If only he had been strangled at birth by his own Rubik snake, there would still be laughter and sanity and conversation in a million American homes.

—Frederick Olsen, *New York Post*, Sept. 8, 1981

In Grand Central Station Mr. James Spence started twisting and turning his brightly colored new racing Cube. A crowd soon gathered around him and followed him on to the train to White Plains — only to leap off in the nick of time after realizing they were on the wrong train.

A school football game in Connecticut was delayed when one player, Bob Blake, failed to take to field with his team. He was found in the dressing room playing with his Cube.

There are endless types of Cubes. Racing, miniature, Royal Wedding Cubes, feminist Cubes, Cube globes, and Braille Cubes. A new type is the

Clinch Cube, specially constructed for honeymoon couples: "a Cube containing two interlocking pieces with brass hinges."

In West Germany two new professions have emerged: Cube marriage counsellors for couples hopelessly addicted to the Cube, and Cube brokers who charge Cubists for solving the problem of the Cube.

There is a new Cube illness: Cubist's thumb, an infection of the thumb, a "localized, exquisitely tender swelling" on the base of the thumb, first diagnosed as gout. This new illness is now officially recognized by the *New England Journal of Medicine*.

A Musical Interlude
Mr. Rubik
(by Robin S. White and Peter Langford)

(Spoken) *Welcome my son. And what brings thee*
to the gates of heaven?
Well it started like this —
About a month ago I got a phone call
from a friend
He said that he was desperate, could I
lend him a hand
I was shocked to see him, he was
babbling like a boob
He'd spent a week inside his house
alone with Rubik's Cube

CHORUS: *Mr. Rubik Rubik Rubik*
Is your Cube from outer space?

Mr. Rubik Rubik Rubik
He got three sides then lost his place
Mr. Rubik Rubik Rubik
He just twists your cube all day
This ain't my idea of child's play

Being the kind of guy I am, I told him I
would try
To help him solve the secrets of the
Cube that made him cry
Well that was thirty days ago and half a
million moves
My wife's all black and blue 'cos I keep
dreaming she's a cube

CHORUS: *Mr. Rubik Rubik Rubik*
What have you got against the sane
Mr. Rubik Rubik Rubik
Is that some kind of Russian game?
Mr. Rubik Rubik Rubik
I think I'll sue for therapy
Your Cube's a mystery to me

I think I've got the answer, all I need's a
little paint
To change the colors of the squares
before I'm in restraint
If that don't work I've got the tools to
force them into place
Before the world goes crazy, I will save
the human race

CHORUS: *Mr. Rubik Rubik Rubik*
My knuckles have gone numb
Mr. Rubik Rubik Rubik
There's no skin left on my thumb

Mr. Rubik Rubik Rubik
What did I ever do to you?
All I need is a little clue

Mr. Rubik Rubik Rubik
It's reduced me down to tears
Mr. Rubik Rubik Rubik
And I've been color-blind for years
Mr. Rubik Rubik Rubik
I think I'm through
All I need is a little clue

Mr. Rubik Rubik Rubik
I can't take it anymore
Mr. Rubik Rubik Rubik
I think I'd rather go to war
Mr. Rubik Rubik Rubik
I'm cracking up, I think I'm gone

(Spoken) Come in my son. Welcome to the
kingdom.
Hey, it's really nice up here. What do
you guys do all day?
Well, we play these . . . .

4

HOW TO RECOGNIZE A CUBAHOLIC

SYMPTOMS

1. The Rubik Twitch. One of the early giveaway signs that Cubaholism is beginning to wreak its terrible price upon the personality is an intolerable shaking of the hands: *the Rubik Twitch*. Even when there is no Cube in sight the hands of the sufferer continually gyrate as if shaking an imaginary cocktail. During this alarming spasm the

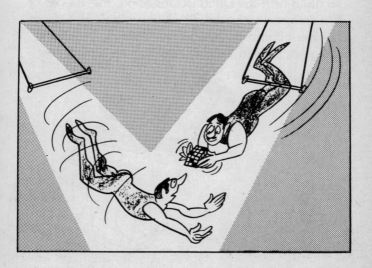

sufferer's eyes are fixed upon his hands with an expression of forlorn hope. If roused from this trancelike state, the sufferer is apt to excuse his behavior by some pathetic ruse: "I must have been dreaming I was strangling a cat," or "I find it exercises my wrists." With a sheepish grin the unfortunate addict usually finds an excuse to slink off to unearth a secret hoard of Cubes, and will be found half an hour later locked in the bathroom feverishly twiddling. The signs are there: urgent action is required if an alarming downhill slide is to be avoided.

2. The Cubic Dream. More and more psychoanalysts have come forward to reveal details of nightmares associated with advanced cases of Cube addition. Often these dreams are presaged by a feeling of nameless dread, somewhat like that produced by an unexpected letter from the IRS. As so often with the Unconscious Mind, the images of the dream may be wreathed in symbolism. One of the most common is a dream in which the patient imagines he is in a garden digging up a plant that

he knows instinctively will kill him. As the soil falls from the herb, the underground part of the plant is seen to consist almost entirely of Cubes (psychologists have referred to these as Cube roots); the patient wakes in a cold sweat, often accompanied by the Rubik twitch. Sometimes the dream is more blatant. The patient may be pursued by huge multicolored Cubes on spindly legs. The only escape lies through a door, but the door is locked by a padlock that can only be unlocked by — yes — solving the Cube dangling from it . . .

3. Hallucinations. The advanced cubaholic begins to see *Cubes* everywhere, even during his waking hours. The skyscraper appears to twiddle and gyrate before his feverish eyes, the child's innocent toy bricks take on a sinister rotating mathematical presence. Such Cubaholics often freak out in public. One was recently arrested for trying to turn around the top of an apartment house: when arrested he said he "was only trying

to make the colors match." When he was placed under arrest in a (cube-shaped) prison block, his nightmare was complete; he had finally been consumed by the Cube.

Fortunately, now that the disease has been recognized, the cure is also at hand. To confess the condition is the first stage toward recovery. There is a 2 percent chance that a Cubaholic can be reclaimed even at this advanced stage of addiction, and for those in the earlier stages chances are even greater. YES, IT IS POSSIBLE TO BEAT THE CUBE — NOT BY TRYING TO SOLVE IT, BUT BY ACCEPTING ITS IMPOSSIBILITY.

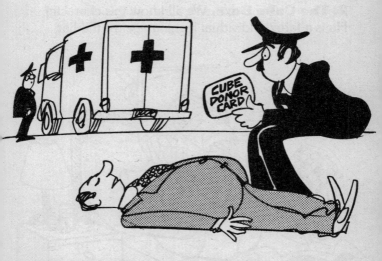

Different Kinds of Cubaholics

1. The Mathematical Wizard. This kind of Cubaholic is often found in attic rooms and corners of small public libraries. He is often very young, with stooping shoulders caused by reading treatises on Advanced Topology. His hair is unkempt, and he is frequently surrounded by little tufts of it, scattered during bouts of frenzied plucking at his head. He is convinced that by study alone he can unlock the secret of rational solution of the cube. His emaciated condition attests to the grip that the so-called toy has established over his otherwise rational mind. Advanced Rubik Twitch often renders his grasp upon his propelling pencil uncertain, and his hands are always wandering toward a much-handled Cube to test the latest of his theories. These always fail.

2. The Cube Bore. We all know this character. He is a faded individual leaning against the bar,

gripping all strangers that pass within earshot with stories of Cube derring-do. There is the "how I can solve any Cube within three minutes" story, or the "how I am the only man ever to have done the Cube while hang-gliding" tale. He is shunned even by those whose addiction to the Cube has already turned them into social pariahs. Cube addicts in the early stages are apt to pass him by with knowing winks. They know that his stories are only wish fulfillment, designed to cover up months of total failure to solve *any* Cube. Each night the unfortunate Bore staggers off to his lonely room bestrewn with unsolved Cubes.

3. The Festooned Addict. This individual tries to turn his addiction into a virtue by advertising it. He or she pretends that Cubes are *fun* by covering their anatomy with dozens of the objects: Cube earrings, Cube tiepins, big Cubes hanging from watch chains, small Cubes dangling from wristwatches. Their pockets bulge with all manner of Cubes. Ladies have little Cubes nestling in their cleavage. All this bravado covers up a dependence on the Cube as pathetic as that of the

mathematical wizard. The ultimate expression of this kind of addiction was a lady in California who went around *dressed as a Cube,* with only her head and legs projecting from the construction. Unfortunately, the secret of unlocking this particular cube proved as intractable as all others, and only a power saw saved her from a Cubic grave.

4. The Furtive Cube Peeper. The secret Cubaholic is one of the most difficult to recognize. He will go to great lengths to conceal the nature of his addiction from the eyes of the world. Typically, he will dress carefully in the sober attire of a businessman, keeping his hands in his pockets to conceal the ravages of the Rubik Twitch. He will sneak off to the john for a secret twiddle, even before breakfast. On train journeys he will keep his cube hidden inside the hollowed-out center of one of the novels of Saul Bellow. His well-padded suits will contain little hip Cubes for a secret bout of twiddling when no one is looking. Often his family and friends are the last to know. They may attribute the faraway look in his eyes and his spinning pupils to overwork or adultery. He will frequently deny his condition, claiming that his Cube practice is not anything more than a social habit, or necessary for ingratiating himself with the boss. When discovery does come, the collapse is often total. The secret Cubaholic will suddenly drop all pretense and start fiddling with his obsession before the breakfast dishes are cleared away. He will stop going to the office, taking

himself instead to a park bench where he will spend all day at furtive twiddling inside a brown paper bag. At this stage he will have nearly reached the ultimate stage, which is...

5. The No-Hoper (or Cubo). The sad and inexorable end of cube addiction: entreaties of husbands, wives, or children are useless against the fascination of the Cube. The sad addict stumbles off, frequently only with the clothes on his back and a suitcase containing his Cubes, to indulge his habit inside bus shelters and other hidden places. Unheeding members of the public step past the prostrate bodies, scarcely noticing the pain-racked expressions and the terrible ravages of DT's (*Delerium Twiddlens*). The Cubo will eventually find himself on Skid Block. There, a strange kind of camaraderie prevails among similar addicts. He will be offered a pull at somebody else's Cube when he is too weak to work his own. Only the ministrations of the Salvation Army keep body and soul together. THIS SHOULD NOT HAPPEN TO YOU.

5

HOW TO LIVE
WITH A CUBAHOLIC

Sooner or later the terrible truth dawns: My husband/wife/boyfriend/son/daughter is a Cubaholic!

Once you have realized this, it is no use burying your head in the sand, hoping that the addiction is a passing fad, like collecting beer cans or Blondie buttons. You have to be aware that you

are fighting an enemy that may be BIGGER THAN BOTH OF YOU, a rotating tyrant that could ruin your lives. You have to fight back. If you cannot persuade your family addict to sign on with Cubaholics Anonymous, you have to undertake the long lonely battle to wean him/her off at home. In our experience there is nothing that tests the warmth and love of the family more than having to cope with a Cube addict in the home. The most everyday situations become fraught with danger: the offer of "taking the dog for a walk" may lead to an orgy of twiddling in hidden back alleys; an innocent bout of "working in the garden" may lead to the exhumation of buried Cubes, revealed only by the ravaged countenance of the digger on his return from the flowerbeds. There is no end to the ingenuity the addict will resort to to satisfy his craving. This chapter lays down a few guidelines for the brave souls who are coping with this dangerous habit without the help of DECUBIFICATION CENTERS.

Concealed Cubes

One of the most common problems you will have to cope with is the concealed Cube syndrome. The addict hides Cubes all around the house and garden. His or her apparent abstinence is only a front for secret indulgence. Those rustling sounds in the cellar in the small hours will be found to be the result of Cubes having been hidden beneath those old stacks of *National Geographic*. Your duty is to SEEK OUT THE CUBES AND DESTROY THEM.

Here are some of the common hiding places that have been named in the CRAP (Cube Rehabilitation Addiction Program) report.

1. The Toilet Tank. An old favorite. Trouble with flushing may give the secret away. A Cube is attached to the ballcock wrapped inside a plastic bag. Be suspicious of intestinal afflictions with a Cubaholic. The john is one of the few places where he can be sure of a quiet uninterrupted session away from prying eyes. Always be wary of square toilet paper holders. One case history even records the false-bottomed bidet, and it is not unknown to find Cubes dangling from those overflow pipes —check them all.

2. Kitchen Cube. The kitchen is swarming with places to hide cubes. Some of these are fairly obvious—the ice-cube tray is an old favorite for the handy pocket versions. Have you checked the cookie jar lately? One other hiding place was only discovered when several cooked Cubes rose to the top of a pot of beef stock.

3. The Living Room. Check the bookcase. Hollowed-out commemorative Bibles are particularly popular because they are fat and nobody ever takes them off the shelf. Is that old chair lumpier than it used to be? Have you taken down the hideous vase of Auntie Margery's from the top shelf to see if it rattles? These are just a few of the places the ingenious Cubaholic may conceal his Cubes. Look out for Cubic rocks in the goldfish bowl. And more than one smoking fireplace has revealed a stash of Cubes up the chimney.

4. The Garden. A veritable hotbed of Cube concealment. The simplest method is burial. You can train your dog to sniff out and retrieve buried Cubes. Make sure your dog is not a Cubaholic first, of course. It is quite common to find Cubes dangling from apple trees among the ripe fruit.

6

HOW TO
KICK THE HABIT

Once you have acknowledged that you are addicted, there is only one course of action: you have to kick the habit. Otherwise you may wind up beyond help, totally twiddled out. Do not kid yourself that giving up your Cube will be easy. Many a broken marriage has been punctuated by promises of reform followed by relapses into worse twiddling than ever. If you are suffering from acute Cubic poisoning, you may be admitted to one of

the special Cube wards in the decubification
centers springing up in some of the major cities.
Here they will "ease you off," using one of the new
drugs like Cubathene or 2-4-5 Isocubathyramol.
This often produces a dramatic physical
improvement—loss of rubik palsy, reduction in
spinning eyeball etc.—but, unfortunately, does not
tackle the root of the problem, the psychological
one. Why do you need to become enslaved to the
Cube in the first place? Do you find it easier to
relate to Cubes than to people? Are you a born
twiddler?

A better method is one of *self-help*.
Particularly if you are supported by family and
friends, this is more likely to lead to a permanent
cure. We have investigated a number of different
methods; we list the most successful here. Once
you have broken the spell, you can kill your Cube
by one of the methods described in the next
chapter.

1. Total Abstinence. This is the most difficult
method, but the most effective. Sudden and
complete cessation of twiddling is probably
impossible for many addicts, but a few
strong-willed ones can manage it. We have even
heard of one man who continued to carry a Cube
in his pocket—a scrambled one! — just to show
that he was no longer subject to temptation. This
method is helped if the addict takes up some
strenuous alternative activity where twiddling is
impossible. Mountain climbing is popular, but we
have heard of at least one fatal accident on the
Eiger because a climber was unable to resist a

quick twiddle while halfway up the North Face in a snowstorm.

2. The Madhouse Method. This one works by driving the addict to such lengths of frustration that he forswears the Cube forever. Special colored stickers are stuck to the Cubies so that the monster really does become unsolvable. This method works for those who have convinced themselves that they have evolved a secret for solving the Cube. The cure usually takes from three to six weeks. The addict is admitted to the hospital in a state of complete exhaustion; by this time his brain, as well as the Cube, is totally scrambled. After he has recovered, even the sight of a Cube is liable to induce the most alarming symptoms. Herein lies a slight danger. One reformed Cubo jumped under an oncoming train at the sight of a nine-year-old twiddler busy at the station.

3. Aversion Therapy. The addict is strapped to a chair with electrodes on his twiddling fingers. He is shown pictures of beautiful Cubes on the way to solution, but every time his fingers begin to twitch he is given a powerful electric shock. After a while he begins to associate Cubes with *pain.* The theory is that he will never want to play the Cube again after a few weeks of this treatment. The only snag is that occasionally it produces the *masochistic Cubaholic*: the unfortunate addict gets to *like* the pain that doing the Cube induces. Like most Cube players, he is probably something of a masochist to start with.

If all these methods fail, the best recourse is

some sort of group therapy. Patients are encouraged to talk out their problems with others who have been through the same traumas and pleasures. Ultimately they are able to make a complete break. Many addicts feel that there is some sort of stigma attached to hospitalization, and for them the best available treatment is to become a member of Cubaholics Anonymous (CA).

Cubaholics Anonymous

Cubaholics Anonymous is an entirely voluntary organization to help Cubos kick the habit. The orgainzation was founded in 1980 by Augustus Judd, a self-confessed Cubomaniac who once boasted of knocking off a dozen or more Cubes before lunch (and that usually a Cubic one).

Reformed Cubaholics address audiences about their Cube habits in an encouraging atmosphere. Eventually people get enough courage to stand up and confess, "I am a Cubaholic." Then they are able to tell the story of their gradual enslavement to this apparently harmless toy. They explain that, while there are many people who seem to be able to take it or leave it, they were one of the unlucky ones for whom Cubes became a way of life. Stories of the heartbreaking degradation are commonplace at these meetings, and will be greeted by murmurs of sympathy from the audience. The sufferer will be given new heart that he is *capable* of breaking the habit with the backup of the organization. From then on, the road to recovery is in sight.

His new friends at CA will be there to help him in times of crisis. As reformed Cubos themselves, they understand those moments of weakness, when reaching for the Cube seems the easiest answer to life's problems. They will sympathize with that overwhelming feeling of "one last twiddle" that has led many a nearly recovered

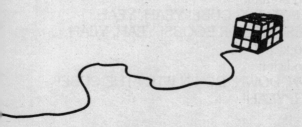

Cubaholic into one last, desperate binge of fruitless twiddling. At the meetings the accounts of relapses by reformed Cubaholics will give support to those who find the final relinquishing of the object that has for such a long time been their main reason for living, such a struggle.

Happily, the CA seems to be making some inroads into the alarming growth of Cube addiction, particularly among the young. There is a growing band of ex-Cubos willing to devote their time to helping others. New members are encouraged to leave their cubes in a garbage chute by the door. A "cure" is officially acknowledged by detonating the sufferer's favorite Cube with a small charge of dynamite. All the meetings finish with a rousing chorus of the CA Anthem, "We Hate the Cube".

First you grab it
Then you twist it
Got the habit
Then you missed it
Got to shake it
Got to break it
WE HATE THE CUBE! YEAH, YEAH.
CUBES ARE FOR BOOBS! YEAH, YEAH.
Got to kick it
Got to lick it
DOWN, DOWN, DOWN WITH THE CUBE!
YEAH! YEAH!

7

HOW TO
KILL THE CUBE

When you are on the road to recovery, you have to make the momentous decision: *NOW is the time to get rid of my Cube (or Cubes).* Do not fool yourself that it will be enough to stick the Cube into some forgotten drawer along with the baggy sweater your mother knitted for you a decade ago. Cubes have a habit of jumping out and creeping around the house at night, so that you find them on the kitchen table in the morning just when you were used to having your first twiddle of the day. We have even known cases where Cubes jettisoned into the garbage have mysteriously

reappeared in the john when the reformed sufferer was thinking about private twiddling sessions in the unreformed days. No, a Cube has to be *killed*, utterly destroyed, reduced first to Cubies and then to powder. Only then will they not return from the dead to haunt their former owner.

There are many different opinions about the best way to kill your Cube. Some favor the *primitive violence* approach. They want to struggle with their Cube in hand-to-hand combat. Very often they choose a large hammer as the weapon. It is true that if you can completely destroy your Cubes in this fashion, you are almost certainly cured *forever*. But there are dangers. Many an ex-Cubaholic has been overcome with remorse as the first Cubie is chipped. Before you can say "Rubik's finger" he has glued it back together again and is twiddling away more frantically than ever.

Personally we favor *The Final Solution*. (Ha ha.)

In this method the Cube is involved in some *total catastrophe* from which it has absolutely no chance of survival.

Here are a few of our suggestions:

1. Deep Burial. We mean *deep* burial. It is absolutely no use digging a little scoop under one of the rose bushes and popping the Cube in there. In the morning you will find it sitting in the middle of your lawn looking irresistibly disheveled. . . . No, Cubes have to be buried at the bottom of *enormously deep holes.* Suitable sites are where they are excavating the foundations of large

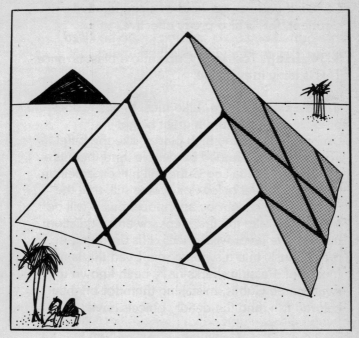

The Egyptian Cube

buildings or digging out bank vaults. We have never heard of a case of a Cube escaping such incarceration — although whenever a skyscraper collapses, we have our suspicions . . .

2. The Irreparable Crush. Dispose of your Cube by crushing it to dust. Few things are strong enough to accomplish this. For example, it is no use tossing your Cube on to the fast lane of a busy highway — they seem to be able to survive for days like this. However, the old-fashioned *steamroller* seems to be able to finish off most

Cubes. If you can get hold of a cooperative elephant, this is also pretty effective.

3. Melting. Toss your Cube into a blast furnace. This is fairly irrevocable.

4. The Long Drop. Like most things, Cubes break if dropped from a great height. Unfortunately many high places, like the Eiffel Tower, are surrounded by people, and there is a danger that the falling Cube will hit some person hundreds of feet below, or, worse still, that the Cube will be caught by an innocent who will be tempted to take the first steps towards addiction himself. We favor wild, sheer cliffs dropping precipitously into a swirling sea. Even this is not foolproof. Passing sharks have been known to swallow the Cubes, mistaking them for brightly colored fish, and the deadly objects have

reappeared themselves weeks later. Deep mineshafts are also a good idea, but an occasional Cubaholic has plunged to his death because of his reluctance to let go of his Cube after he has thrown it into the hole.

5. Destructacube Inc. This new organization, founded only recently after the threat of the Cube was recognized, bravely offers to take on the responsibility for destroying Cubes. Owners simply send their Cubes (with a check or money order for $25) to Destructacube, P.O. Box 216, Wheeling, West Virginia. The Cubes are never heard of again. Rumors that the Cubes are simply polished up a bit and resold to schoolgirl innocents are, we believe, entirely erroneous.

6. Explosion. High explosives can often get rid of Cubes. Hurling them into quarries during blasting operations is a good idea.

7. Cubes into Space. Perhaps the long-term solution to Cube infestation. We visualize cargos of Cubes thrown up beyond the atmosphere. They will circle the earth well beyond twiddling distance — or if they reenter the atmosphere, they will burn up. There may be a danger to astronauts of Close Encounters of the Cubic Kind.

8. Natural Disasters. Tidal waves, earth-quakes, and volcanic eruptions will probably result in the destruction of large numbers of Cubes. There is some speculation among biblical scholars that the Cube was discovered long ago in Sodom and Gomorrah — perhaps Rubik's Rattlesnake was implicated in their untimely destruction.

Once your Cube is dead, you will be FREE. Make sure you have rooted out every last one; suddenly discovering a forgotton old Cube in the back of a cupboard can be *disastrous*.

Just think, the death of your Cube means you can return to normal life. You can play with your kids again; or, if you are a kid, you can play with your parents again. You can watch TV once more. You can reintroduce yourself to your old friends. But be careful to avoid the company of other Cubaholics for a long time — even a handshake with one of these can lead to an unwary twiddle, especially if they are suffering from Rubik's Palsy.

THE ONLY GOOD CUBE IS A DEAD CUBE.

8

CUBES ARE
FOR SQUARES

One important aspect of our campaign to eliminate the Cube from its present overweaning position in society is to make the Cube unfashionable. At the moment the 0.0001 percent of the population who can *solve* the Cube are treated like demigods. All this must stop. We aim to make the Cube seem an undesirable and despicable object. Those who indulge in it should seem tainted by the

association. This will not be easy: some people still have the mistaken idea that the Cube is a harmless toy. However, our new pressure group, CAMP (Cubes Are Malicious Pests), aims to reverse these attitudes. We plan a two-pronged attack. First, we have hired the prestigious advertising agency of Twitchi & Twitchi — most of its staff are reformed Cubaholics. Second, we are planning to influence public opinion against the Cube by a series of demonstrations and Ban the Cube marches, led by a number of prominent public figures. These will include citizens of the caliber of Lee Iacocca and Ann Landers, who has been receiving letters from Cubaholics for the past three years.

Twitchi & Twitchi are also planning a series of TV advertisements that will emphasize the antisocial nature of Cube addiction, as well as its health hazards.

1. A beautiful girl and a handsome man are seen wandering along a palm-fringed beach in an exotic location. The sun sets over opalescent waves; violins play romantic music. As they turn for the clinch, you suddenly see that the man is totally absorbed in solving his Cube. The girl hits him over the head with a coconut and stomps off. Insinuating voiceover says, "You lose more than your marbles if you're Cubic."

2. The ad opens with a panning shot around one of those exclusive restaurants that usually demonstrate the merits of credit cards. Attractive women dine with sleek-looking executives on lobster and caviar to soft music and the murmur of

civilized chatter. The camera eventually takes in a sign that says "NO CUBES PERMITTED." Beyond lies another sign that instructs "CUBE USERS THIS WAY." As the camera tracks towards the second dining room, we hear the sounds of breaking china and slobbering. Finally, the pathetic creatures are revealed: hands shaking from Rubik Twitch, soup dribbling down stubbly chins, great gobs of custard flying this way and that — need we say more? The voiceover says, simply: "Are YOU a Cubic eater?"

3. The scene is a crowded railway station. As the train draws in we see that it is divided into two kinds of cars: "Cubes permitted" and "No Twiddling." Nice, well-scrubbed, middle class families are seen getting into the latter, where they join gray-haired gentlemen doing the *Times* crossword puzzle and matrons with Saks shopping bags. Then we cut to the other car; it is full of an

array of unkempt loonies, all desperately trying to solve their Cubes. One of them falls to the floor in a coma. The voiceover says: "Do YOU travel with the right kind of people?"

4. A road accident. Twisted wrecks of cars lie in a confused mass; flashing ambulance lights illuminate the nighttime scene. An old-fashioned policeman — the kind with a strong, lined face, at once worldly and compassionate — is probing round inside one of the cars, where we catch a glimpse of a limp body. Suddenly, the cop looks up significantly and nods in a sad and knowing way. There, on the floor of the car, lies a Rubik Cube. As the scene fades, we hear the words: "Rubik's Cubes and driving don't mix."

With these images implanted on the collective brain, we anticipate that the spread of the Cube will be prevented, or at least temporarily halted. The Rotary Club will probably change its name.

As this "Down with the Cube" attitude spreads, more and more anti-Cube phrases will spring to people's lips. "Oh, ignore him, he's just a Cube-head," they will say. Or, "Poor Mildred, George is home again with another attack of the Rubiks" will be overheard in the supermarket. "Your eyes look positively *Cubic*" will describe a feverish condition.

In this way the world will be divided into the normals and the Cube players. The latter will become more and more ashamed of their dangerous obsession. Soon it will be hard to find any sign of public twiddling. Cubes will have been driven underground into dimly lit dives, silent except for the "click-click-click" of addicts still at it, and the occasional stifled groan as the solution fails to come out yet again.

Closet Cubos will describe the normals as "sphericals." They may fight back in a desultory way with "Cube Is Good" campaigns, or "We'd rather be Cubic than straight" buttons. But the battle for public opinion will have been lost. Cubes will become square.

9

THE CUBIC WORLD: A HORROR STORY

We have a vision of what the world would be like if the Cube really did take over. You may find this too horrible to contemplate, yet it *could* happen if the present tide of Cubes continued to grow exponentially. Life would become dominated by Cubes from the cradle to the grave.

Soon after babies left the hospital they would be given their first Cubes. Rattles would have

Cubic heads. Rubik's dolls would be composed of little bits of the human anatomy that have to be twiddled around to get them back to humanoid appearance. Growth and progress would be rewarded by bigger and better Cubes, until at eighteen the child would be given the "key to the Cube," and see for the first time what an

unscrambled Rubik looks like. At this age the youth
or girl would be able to solve the Cube of his or
her choice without parental consent. Fond
grandparents would soon look forward to the rattle
of tiny Cubes, and the cycle (or more correctly the
Cubicle) of the generations would be complete.

By this time architecture would be dominated
by the Cube. All new houses would be identi-
cal Cubes, decorated in red, yellow, green,
white, or blue Cubies, which could be detached
and rearranged every spring. Because,

as we all know by now, there are more than
15,000,000,000,000,000 ways of arranging the
Cubies, no two houses would be the same.
People's status would be rewarded by permitting
progressively unscrambled houses, but only the
president would be allowed a wholly unscrambled
domain. The White House would be renamed the
Red, Green, White, Yellow, and Blue House.

Cubism would be the only form of painting
from the past acknowledged by the new regime.
New paintings would be entirely of Cubes. Books
will be printed on the sides of Cubes, which people
would have to unscramble to read. This way, it
would take a lifetime to read the *Adventures of
Peter Rabbit*. On Sunday the populace would
stream off to St. Rubik's, where they would be
harangued on the iniquity of spheres and read
passages from the *First Book of Permutations and
Combinations*. Most ball games would have been
abolished by now (spheres being immoral), but a
few will be modified so that they can be played
with square balls. Sunday afternoons will thus be a
dreary time for most people, although gardeners

can amuse themselves in the vegetable plot with trying to grow the new Cubic potatoes, tomatoes, and cubicumbers.

In the evenings the average family will retire to the living cube, where they will attempt to solve the Cubic chairs into a comfortable position (out of 345,000,000 possible positions, only one is comfortable). They will then switch on the Cube, when they will be able to see a succession of boring programs — situation comedies about funny combinations of colors, or talk shows on which aging *Cubemeisters* attempt to reconstruct the plays that made them famous. And so to Cubic bed, which may take quite a time to twist around so that the pillows are all up at one end.

Politics will have become Cubic too. There will only be six possible opinions on any issue, and the fifty-four voting politicians will all rush around to see if they can finish up on the same side. Wars, of course, will still be fought — by intercontinental ballistic Cube.

Most manufacturing industry will be linked to producing Cubes or Cube derivatives. The Japanese will lead the world in Cubes that are faster, smaller, and cheaper than anyone else's. British Cubes, though well made, will suffer a chronic shortage of spare parts; the Swiss Cube will have diamond bearings and will be the best long-term investment. Third World nations will have a dangerous shortage of Cubes, particularly after devastating natural disasters like floods. Voluntary organizations such as the International Red Cube will go some way toward remedying this.

The life of the man in the street will be much the same. The abolition of the wheel will cause a few problems at first, and somehow the invention of ratchet-shaped roads will never entirely remove the vibration problems associated with Cubic wheels. Cubic money may pose some difficulties, but most financial transactions can be performed with a single Cube, although it will habitually take several hours to twiddle the Cube around to the right position for the spare change in the deal. Cubic society will be so preoccupied with trying to work out such problems that there will be few disturbances, although at first a few revolutionary groups may meet in secret to show contraband pictures of spheres. Life will become one long twiddle.

Two horrible to believe? Yet this could be the kind of world we will inherit if the action advocated in this book is not implemented NOW.

10

BRAVE NEW CUBE-FREE WORLD

Once the population has been weaned from the Cube, all forms of Cubism will become abhorrent. People will not want to be reminded of their addicted days. The Cube will be *eliminated from*

society. Just imagine this paradise on earth! No more square skyscrapers — their shape, and the multitude of glistening windows, are too reminiscent of Rubik's nightmare. They will be replaced by tall buildings in the shape of mushrooms or bananas. Architecture will reach new heights in the attempt to avoid any suggestion of a corner. Housing will become transformed: no longer will people complain of living in modern "boxes" — these will be outlawed. Houses will be shaped like igloos, tortoises, or goldfish. The tyranny of the Cube will be gone forever.

The Cube-free world will permeate our everyday lives. Nothing that allows nostalgia for the days of incessant twiddling will be permitted. Cube inspectors will pass from door to door to make sure that all new households are purged of any Cubic associations. TV sets will be redesigned to look like hot dogs. Bread will be octagonal. Anything with cubic form will be replaced by the circle, the star, the swirling shapes of nature, or an irregular blob.

The beady eye of the Cube inspector will light upon the ice-cube tray, where for generations ice has been manufactured in the shape of sinful Cubes. These will be replaced by small replicas of the Astrodome or the Jefferson Monument. Sugar cubes will be replaced by imaginative reproductions of Mickey Mouse and Pluto.

The revolution in shapes of everyday objects will be matched by an aesthetic revolution. Ruskin's famous edict "Nature abhors the Cube" will be learned at school along with the alphabet, which fortunately does not include any cubic letters. The ideal circular city will be designed where all straight lines are avoided and men travel to their work in spherical vehicles to sit at desks shaped like strawberries. Secretaries will take notes on circular notepads. The squash court will be redesigned will a series of organic protruberances that will make return of the ball impossible. All beds will be heart-shaped. Children will be given toy bricks in odd shapes from which it will be impossible to build a tower. By the end of the century, the word *Cube* will have passed from the language forever.

The last Rubik's Cube will be kept in a vault in a museum under lock and key, where it will be studied by scholars writing the history of the fever that nearly destroyed Civilization As We Know It.

The future is entirely circular.

Or is it? . . .